Charles E. Mann

In the heart of Cape Ann

The story of Dogtown

Charles E. Mann

In the heart of Cape Ann
The story of Dogtown

ISBN/EAN: 9783744735186

Printed in Europe, USA, Canada, Australia, Japan

Cover: Foto ©Thomas Meinert / pixelio.de

More available books at **www.hansebooks.com**

IN THE

HEART

OF CAPE ANN

OR THE

STORY OF DOGTOWN

BY

CHARLES E. MANN

With Illustrations by Catherine M. Follansbee

GLOUCESTER, MASS. :

PROCTER BROTHERS. PUBLISHERS

108 MAIN STREET

5 A|

DOGTOWN.

□ HOUSES,
■ CELLARS.
DRAWN BY CHARLES E. MANN

PREFATORY NOTE.

These Dogtown Sketches were written almost
wholly as the result of an effort to satisfy the curiosity
of the author as to the history, biography and traditions of the deserted village, their continuation and
publication being encouraged by the general attention they commanded. It is not claimed that they
are complete, but it is believed they contain far more
information than has yet been published concerning
their subject. The writer desires to express his deep
sense of obligation to those who, before the publication of the matter originally prepared, and since,
have assisted by furnishing facts and reminiscences.

They have made it possible to get together a mass of authentic history, where at first it seemed that at best, only a few traditions were to be rescued from oblivion. Of course nearly all the material is in the memories of Cape Ann's aged people, and it has been a source of unalloyed pleasure to sit by them and listen to their discourses upon the days of long ago. Among the precious memories of this year will be those of many an hour spent in ancient kitchens, while sweet-faced old ladies, often with sweeter voices, or men with whitened locks and time-furrowed cheeks, recalled the stories told them by the fireside by other dear old women and noble old men of a past century. No wonder Gloucester has developed into such an admirable and lovable a community, when there still lingers among her people so many of their honored progenitors.

CHAPTER I.

Ever since Goldsmith wrote his "Deserted Village" there has been a weird, poetic and sentimental charm about abandoned settlements, that has so exerted itself over some minds that it has become a pleasure to make the investigations incident to a correct understanding of what manner of men found it convenient or necessary to build habitations which it afterwards became advisable to desert. Archæologists have given lifetimes, almost, to the investigation of the modes of life of the cliff dwellers of Arizona and

New Mexico. There are comparatively few ruined
cities in America; and even more rare are the in-
stances of deserted villages which were once inhabited
by white men, the progenitors of people who are living to-day. It has been the pleasure of the writer
during the past few months to acquaint many people
with their ancestors, in a figurative sense, for in the
heart of Cape Ann may be found a village which
was once inhabited by the grandparents or more dis-
tant progenitors of many who are to-day active in the
affairs of Gloucester and Rockport.

To-day the only inhabitants of "Dogtown" are
lowing kine, an occasional decrepit horse turned out
to pasture as a pensioner, or woodchucks, crows and
migrating birds. Its grass-grown streets are there,
its foot-worn door-stones may be used for a resting-
place by the occasional summer tourist on a tramp
across the cape, a curiosity seeking Appalachian, or by
the more numerous berry pickers. The cleared land
in the midst of such a waste of rocks, as is the rule in
Dogtown Commons, always leads to speculation;
even more suggestive are the walled yards and the
many cellars, both of houses and farm buildings.

Concerning these old cellars novelists have woven
their romances, and poets have sung. Nearly a half-
century ago they excited the interest of Richard

Henry Dana and Thomas Starr King and the circle of rare minds they drew to Cape Ann with them. Long afterwards, Col. Thomas Wentworth Higginson, in one of those delightful bits of reminiscence scattered through "Oldport Days," described a walk to Dogtown Commons from Pigeon Cove:

"What can Hawthorne mean by saying in his English diary that 'an American would never understand the passage in Bunyan about Christian and Hopeful going astray along by a by-path into the grounds of Giant Despair, from there being no stiles and by-paths in our country'? So much of the charm of American pedestrianism lies in the by-paths: For instance, the whole interior of Cape Ann, beyond Gloucester, is a continuous woodland, with granite ledges everywhere cropping out, around which the high-road winds, following the curving and indented line of the sea, and dotted here and there with fishing hamlets. This whole interior is traversed by a network of foot-paths, rarely passable for a wagon, and not always for a horse, but enabling the pedestrian to go from any one of the villages to any other, in a line almost direct, and always under an agreeable shade. By the longest of these hidden ways, one may go from Pigeon Cove to Gloucester, ten miles, without seeing a public road. In the little

inn at the former village there used to hang an old
map of this whole forest region,[1] giving a chart of
some of these paths, which were said to date back to
the first settlement of the country. One of them, for
instance, was called on the map 'Old road from
Sandy Bay to 'Squam Meeting-House through the
Woods'; but the road is now scarcely even a bridle-
path, and the most faithful worshipper could not seek
'Squam meeting-house in the family chaise. These
woods have been lately devastated; but when I first
knew the region, it was as good as any German
forest. Often we stepped from the edge of the sea
into some gap in the woods; there seemed hardly
more than a rabbit-track, yet presently we met some
wayfarer who had crossed the Cape by it.

"A piney dell gave some vista of the broad sea we
were leaving, and an opening in the woods displayed
another blue sea-line before; the encountering breezes
interchanged odors of berry bushes and scent of brine;
penetrating further among oaks and walnuts we came
upon some little cottage, quaint and sheltered as any
Spenser drew; it was not built on the high-road, and
turned its vine-clad gable away from even the foot-
path. Then the ground rose and other breezes came;

---

[1] This is a reference to the "Mason" map of Cape Ann. A copy of it
hangs at the present time in the office of the city clerk.

perhaps we climbed trees to look for landmarks, and found only an unseen quarry. Three miles inland, as I remember, we found the hearthstones of a vanished settlement; then we passed a swamp with cardinal flowers; then a cathedral of noble pines, topped with crows' nests. If we had not gone astray, by this time we would have presently emerged on Dogtown Common, an elevated tableland, overspread with great boulders as with houses, and encircled with a girdle of green woods and another girdle of blue sea. I know of nothing like that gray waste of boulders; it is a natural Salisbury Plain, of which icebergs and ocean currents were the Druidic builders; in that multitude of couchant monsters there seems a sense of suspended life; you feel as if they must speak and answer to each other in the silent nights, but by day only the wandering sea-birds seek them, on their way across the Cape, and the sweet-bay and green fern imbed them in a softer and deeper setting as the years go by. This is the 'height of ground' of that wild foot-path; but as you recede farther from the outer ocean and approach Gloucester, you come among still wilder ledges, unsafe without a guide, and you find in one place a cluster of deserted houses, too difficult of access to remove even their materials, so that they are left to moulder alone. I used to wander in those

woods, summer after summer, till I had made my own
chart of their devious tracks, and now when I close
my eyes in this Oldport midsummer, the soft Italian
air takes on something of a Scandinavian vigor; for
the incessant roll of carriages I hear the tinkle of the
quarryman's hammer and the veery's song; and I long
for those perfumed and breezy pastures, and for those
promontories of granite where the fresh water is nec-
tar and the salt sea has a regal blue."

Col. Higginson hints in the above passage at many
of the topographical and geographical features of the
Heart of Cape Ann. The old road from Sandy Bay
to 'Squam is what is now known as Revere street.
He draws the line between Dogtown village and
Dogtown Commons with as much care as the most
particular old-timer could wish. He also mentions
Lamb or Raccoon ledge, it is difficult to say which.

Dogtown is a pathetic, fascinating place. Why did
more than one hundred families exile themselves from
the life of the villages so near them, and dwell in lone-
liness and often in poverty, in this barren and secluded
spot? The name "Dogtown," it is well understood,
came from the canines kept by the so-called "widows"
of the place, when the evil days came that saw their
natural protectors either in their graves or buried
beneath the ocean.

There are many approaches to Dogtown. I have quoted Col. Higginson's description of the route from Pigeon Cove, by way of the old road from Sandy Bay to the 'Squam church, which is still passable. Coming from 'Squam, one may leave the church, walk a mile through the same road, past the Cape Ann Granite Co.'s quarries, the road passing through the upper end of one, to the house of David Dennison, an ancient gambrel-roofed lean-to, built by Mr. Dennison's first ancestor on Cape Ann, and a fine sample of the better class of the Dogtown homes. From here he can branch off to the right, by the Whale's Jaw, and thence go to the deserted village. The road by Goose Cove, near Riverdale, leads to the same point, the Whale's Jaw, a great boulder split by lightning, or more probably by frost, to resemble the open jaws of a whale. Gee avenue and Stanwood street, in Riverdale, lead past the cellar of Judith Ryon (or Rhines), to that of Abraham Wharf, and thence to the main street of the village.

Persons coming from East Gloucester may, if they are strong on their feet, go up Webster street and enter the pastures by crossing Lamb Ledge—no small task, for it is one of the most wonderful terminal moraines in New England, the boulders being piled one upon another in the most orderly confusion until they

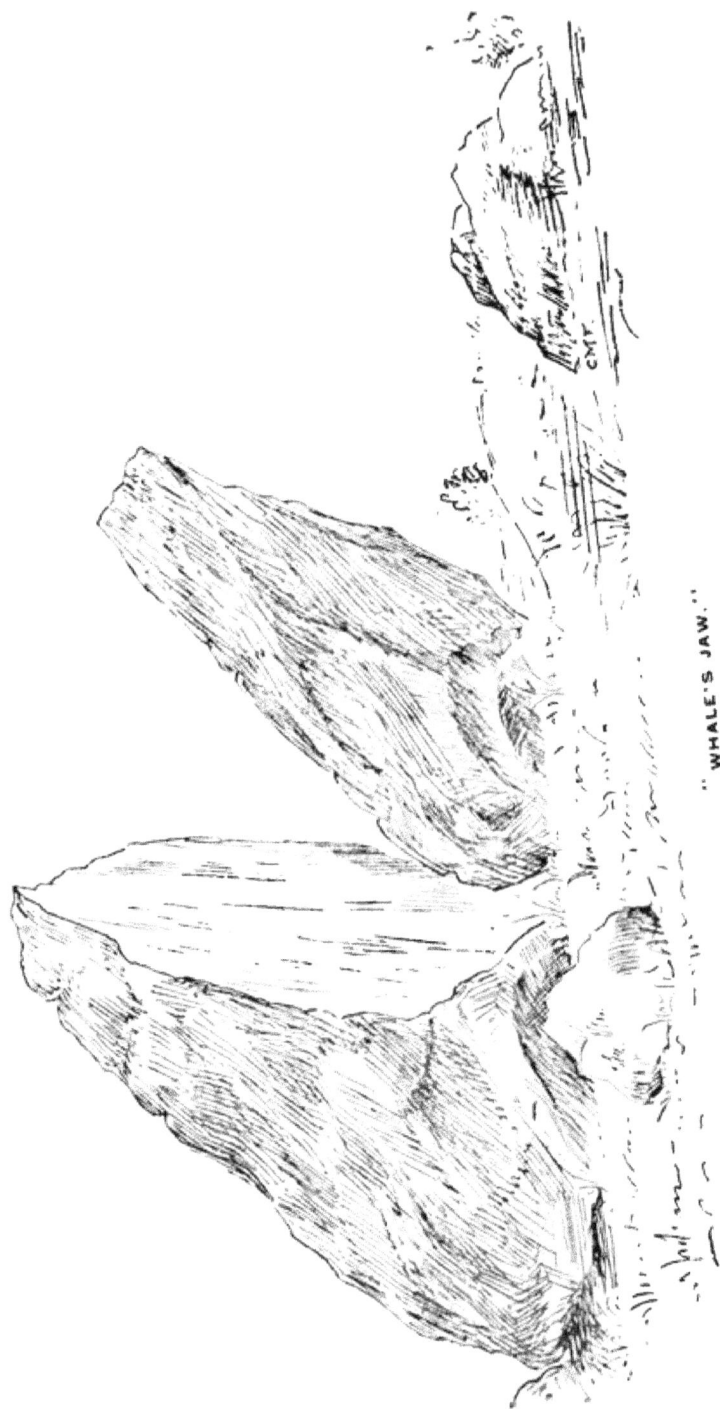

"WHALE'S JAW."

reach the level of the Commons from the deep valley into which some glacier swept them ages ago. It is a good hour's stint to cross the ledge, and then one passes by Railcut Hill, the highest point on the outer Cape, to the old Rockport road, another picturesque and grass-grown highway of olden times, and enters the Pigeon Cove path which continues by the Whale's Jaw at the clearing once occupied by James Witham, son of Thomas and grandson of Henry, the first of the line in this country.

Witham was born in 1693, and built this house at what is known as Stacy's Pines, the location bearing the suggestive title of the "parting path." He engaged in tending flocks for the Low family, for $300 annually, his son Thomas succeeding him in his work. Only the cellar of the house remains. It was in later years a great resort for young people for mirth and jollity until its demolition. The path continues across the valley in which the Gloucester Branch of the Boston & Maine railroad runs, which bears the marks of the tides on its sentinel ledges, showing that once they flowed through here from Good Harbor or Long Beach to the 'Squam river, and thence to the big rock, "Peter's Pulpit," which in the distance looks like a pitch-roofed house, which stands directly on the Dogtown road, marking the end of the main settle-

ment.   The following diagram may give a clearer
idea of the foregoing:

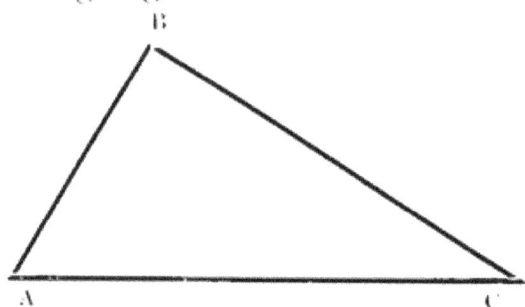

The straight lines in the triangle represent the
general direction of three very crooked roads.   A is
the point on Dogtown road, beyond the intersection
of Reynard and Cherry streets, where the road from
B meets it.   From A the Dogtown road continues up
what old residents of Riverdale call "gravel hill,"
past the Vivian barn, and on to the rock variously
called "Peter's Pulpit," "Pulpit Rock," and "Uncle
Andrew's Rock," at C.   It then winds on to the
Whale's Jaw.   Opposite A is the site of the Nathaniel
Day house.   B is the point where Gee avenue and
Stanwood street meet.   The grass-grown road from
B to C is the "Dogtown Common road," that is, it is
the road over the Common to Dogtown.   That from
A to C is the "Dogtown road," and that from A to B
is paradoxically called the "back road," though it is
nearer civilization than either of the others.   Were
a prize of $50 to be offered a person who would start

from A, go to B, thence to C and back to A without getting off the road, he probably never would receive it. I have been over it many times, and never failed to get lost for a few moments at least. Perhaps the spirit of Peg Wesson, who did not live in Dogtown, of Luce George, or of Judy Rhines, if Judy really was a witch, has bewitched me for the contemplated sacrilege of writing them up.

Practically all the old people agree in calling the roads by the names I have given. The Commons road is also sometimes called the " walled-in " road, as the walls occasionally cross it. Old people do not call the cellars on the latter road—of Morgan Stanwood, Judy Rhines, Moll Jacobs and others in " Dogtown," they are on the " Commons." The reader will probably be incapable of drawing so fine a distinction. There were obvious reasons why people who lived on the Commons road should have chosen to do so.

CHAPTER II.

THE "QUEEN OF THE WITCHES."

The most natural, because the most interesting approach to the village, is by its outpost, the cellar of "Tammy" Younger, the "queen of the witches," at Fox Hill. She was more often seen by the predecessors of this generation on Cape Ann, was better known, and far more respected and feared than any of her confreres. Perhaps the reader will be better able to judge whether the title for two or three generations bestowed on Tammy was deserved, after a careful perusal of this chapter. It is possible that after reading it he may be disposed to transfer the title to her aunt, the redoubtable "Luce George."

Coming from the Harbor village of Gloucester, through Maplewood avenue, one reaches Poplar street, and after turning to the left, soon reaches the bridge at Alewife brook. Beneath a solitary poplar, on a little rise of ground, is the cellar of Tammy Younger. An apple orchard stands near. The cellar has been cleared recently of a growth of sumacs which nearly obscured it. Thomazine Younger was born July 28, 1753, and was the daughter of William Younger, sojourner, and Lucy Foster, who were married on March 6, 1750, by Rev. John White, pastor of the First Church.

A recent writer claims that this house was in later years the resort of buccaneers and lawless men. Fortune telling, card playing and other amusements whiled away their time. Money was found in the cellar after Tammy's death. These assertions are denied by members of her family who still remain, and apparently with good reason.

A friend of the writer was, a few years since, chasing a woodchuck, which went into the cellar. In digging for the animal he unearthed a handsomely ornamented snuff box, the cover bearing a representation of a full rigged ship. It was probably Tammy's, as she is said to have been a snuff taker as well as smoker, but it has been credited to a possible myth-

A TYPICAL DOGTOWN HOUSE.

ical British sea captain who was wont to visit the
house.

Mr. John Low Babson, one of Gloucester's oldest
residents, recalls that in the early twilight of an autum-
nal evening he was going from Fresh Water Cove to
his home, still standing, near the Green in the "up
in town" village, and had to pass through the bury-
ing ground near the bridge. A man was digging
a grave. "Who is that for?" he asked. "Tammy
Younger," the sexton replied. "Is she dead?" was
young Babson's surprised query. "We don't very
often dig graves for folks that aint dead," was the
testy response. Mr. Babson gives a good illustration
of the prevalent impressions concerning Tammy, in
a reminiscence of his boyhood. He was driving home
the cows, past her dwelling, when she came to the
door and accosted him, begging him, with strong
expletives, if he loved her life, to get her a pail
of water. He got it, of course, from the brook
behind the cabin. No one ever refused Tammy.

Mrs. Elizabeth Day, of Wheeler's Point, says that
Tammy died Feb. 4, 1829. She was therefore 76
years old. Mrs. Day's father, John Hodgkins, was
a cabinet maker, who lived in the house just above
the railroad track, on Washington street. Elizabeth
was a child of ten years. For two or three years

Tammy, who often saw her, had taken a fancy to her, and would often ask her to come and live with her at Fox Hill, as she was lonely. Tammy used to make butter and carry it to the Harbor to sell, and whenever she passed along other members of the family would say, "Here comes Aunt Tam to take you up to her house with her." The little girl's heart was thus constantly terrorized with the thought that Tammy would some time capture her, and her feelings may well be imagined when on that stormy winter day word came that Tammy was dead and that Mr. Hodgkins must make her a coffin.

Old Mrs. Pulcifer, whose daughter recently died at a great age, had attended her in her last sickness, and Oliver, Tammy's nephew, who was brought up by her, had deferred to Mrs. Pulcifer's advice as to the funeral arrangements. He said he wanted to do everything that could be done to have things nice, so when advised to have as good a coffin as could be made, with a pure silver plate, he at once ordered it. It was of course thought the thing in those days to have "spirit" on funeral occasions, and in deference to Mrs. Pulcifer's opinion, he ordered no rum, or other cheap liquors, but cordials, wines, and other of the better class of beverages. Mrs. Pulcifer is remembered to have said afterward that her only regret was that she had not ordered the church bells tolled for Tammy, as she was sure it would have been done.

But to return to Mr. Hodgkins and Tammy's coffin. All that rainy day he toiled upon it, and toward night it was ready for polishing. He had a large kitchen, and it was his custom when polishing coffins to bring them into that room, where he had a better chance to work. The children were therefore used to such sights. But on this particular night the storm was so severe that he did not care to risk spoiling his work by taking it back to the shop, so after rubbing it down with beeswax he stood it up in the corner, blew out his candle and said nothing.

Soon bedtime came. The children, sitting by the comfortable open fire in the adjoining room, were warned by their mother to retire: "Come John, it's time for you and Elizabeth to go to bed." John took a candle, and started. It was necessary to go through the kitchen in order to reach the chambers above. As he opened the door, the light of his candle fell on the shiny coffin in the corner. Other people might not believe Tammy was a witch; on that night John was sure she was both a witch and a ghost. He began to whimper, " I won't go to bed with Aunt Tam Younger's coffin in the house," said he. As he drew

back, Elizabeth bravely stepped into the breach, but
one sight of the coffin was enough, and she too, became panicky, and declared that there was no sleep for
her if that coffin was to remain.   Mother impatiently
got up, and boldly threw the door wide open.   She
was never known to be afraid of anything, but a look
unnerved her also, and she joined with the children
and said she would never go to bed with that thing
there.   In vain the father said the rain would spoil
it; it was three against one.   "Spoil it or not," said
the good housewife, "I won't stay in the house with
it."   So "pa" gave in, got a quilt, wrapped it up,
and bore it through the storm to the shop.

Tammy had a square window in the rear of her
house, with a wooden door.   This was kept shut,
there being a long string attached to it, by which
Tammy could open it at will.   The sound of a team
crossing the bridge over the brook was usually a
signal for Tammy to swing open the shutter and
boldly communicate with the driver.   A footstep on
the bridge would also serve to open the window.   If

Tammy asked for a mackerel or any other thing she saw in the hand or the team of a passer-by, she usually got it, or the unlucky traveller got a piece of her mind. On one autumn day a luckless youth passing noticed a big pile of pumpkins sunning against the rear of the house. Crossing the lot to avoid the steep hill, as many do to-day, he thoughtlessly pulled out one, low down in the pile. The effect was unexpected, for at once the whole collection coasted down the hill into the brook. Tammy's window flew open. A torrent of vocal pyrotechnics accompanied the hours of labor that followed, as that unhappy boy fished out the pumpkins, and toiled back and forth up the hill until they were piled up again.

As is well known, a good deal of the land on Dogtown Commons is in the hands of the Younger family. I have said that Oliver Younger was brought up by his aunt, and it seems that he was unaware of the fact that the land belonged to his father and not to her. Many years after his father's death, he was remarking to one of the Allens, a neighbor, what a care his aunt's land was to him, and Allen responded, "Well, it's all yours, anyway. Your father willed it to you, for I signed the will as one of the witnesses." This was news to Oliver, but acting on the hint given he waited an opportunity when Tammy was away, and then ransacked the house. In the secret drawer of a small table, he found the will. Under ordinary circumstances it would have been outlawed, but as this was the first knowledge anyone had of its existence, it was admitted to probate.

While Tammy Younger won for herself a reputation as a woman with a very choice vocabulary, especially in the line of invective, she evidently was "not as bad as she has been painted," as Mr. Benjamin P. Kidder of Rockport says, and his testimony is confirmed by aged Betsey Elwell of Malden, who remembers her well, as well as by Mrs. Almira Riggs, but recently deceased. The truth seems to be that Tammy had an aunt, known by the name of "Luce (Lucy) George." She it was who originally lived in the Fox Hill House, and who used to stand at the door of her cabin and bewitch the oxen so that they would stand with their tongues run out, but could not come up the hill until some of the corn they drew was contributed to her. She, like Peg Wesson, is said to have had the art of so bewitching a load of wood that it would not stay on the ox team until a portion had been unloaded at her door. It is said she would go to the wharves: when the fishing vessels came in, and exact her tribute of fish. Of course these are traditions. but I give them for what they are worth to susceptible minds. Tammy Younger lived with her aunt. Hence the confusion of the two. Tammy was not tall and raw-boned, as some have alleged, but short and inclined to plumpness.

At one time in her life, she decided to part with two rather long teeth that decorated each side of her upper jaw. They were not as long as Black Nell's, which one old lady insists were fully an inch in length, nor as long as "Judy Rhines'," but they were troublesome, so she sent for "Granther Stannard" to act in the capacity of dentist. This must have been before the old gentleman became convinced that his legs were made of glass, and refused to use them, for he went over from his house on the "walled-in way." Tammy seated herself in a chair, and Capt. Stanwood took a firm hold with his nippers and soon a tooth gave way. Being a joker, he only drew it partly down. where it rested in plain sight. against her under lip.   He then drew down the other to exactly the same length. and immediately afterwards announced. that owing to the obstinacy of the teeth. he could do no more for her.   The pen refuses to record the torrent of picturesque language which history alleges was poured upon " Johnny Morgan's " luckless head.   After worrying her awhile, the teeth were taken out.

AN ANCIENT MANTLEPIECE.

CHAPTER III.

FROM FOX HILL OVER THE BACK ROAD.

Nothwithstanding the various theories which have been brought forward to explain the original peopling of Dogtown, and its mysterious decline, the writer believes it may all be traced to a circumstance which is in no sense mysterious, but on the contrary, just what might have been expected. This circumstance was the building of the bridge at Riverdale and the Goose Cove Dam, each making it possible to construct the road on the easterly side of the mill pond, and making what had been the road to Annisquam to the harbor a "back road."

The reader can easily imagine the condition of affairs when the road from the Green northerly led

only to Wheeler's Point. Then he must start from
the Green through what is now Poplar street, turn up
over Fox Hill, and wind down to Gravel Hill and
across the moor to the vicinity of the Castle, and
thence make his way over the hill by the Riggs house
and around Goose Cove.

It will thus be seen that the central village of Dogtown was but a very short distance from the main
road, while what is now Riverdale village is quite
a distance from it. As old people tell us, it was then
"going up into the city" to go to Dogtown. There
was nothing singular at all that under those condi-
tions Dogtown should have thriven, and that when
the building of the bridge and dam occurred, and the
whole tide of travel left this road and went around
the other way, Dogtown languished and died. It
was something like a boom city in the West, which
perishes when the railroad goes elsewhere.

It was the facts that have been stated that gave the
home of Luce George and Tammy Younger such
importance, for almost everybody had to pass it.

Just beyond the cellar of Tammy Younger, after
the turn in the road which brings one in sight of Riverdale, is the cellar of the first blacksmith in town,
lying beside the travelled road, but still in the road-
way. Here stood the shop of Joseph Allen, who

came to Gloucester in 1674, being encouraged to settle by grants of land and a common right. He had two wives and seventeen children. One of the children, also named Joseph, became very wealthy, his home being on Poplar street, near the house occupied by Mr. Joseph A. Procter.

I think the blacksmith shop must have stood by the cellar, and the cellar have been that of the house, built perhaps by Allen, but known within the memory of persons now living as the "Noble" house, the Nobles being ancestors of numerous Riverdale people.

The white cottage facing up the road immediately beyond is on the site of another old mansion which was standing before the back road became disused, Aunt Pamelia Allen being its occupant. Where the Tracy greenhouses are now located, opposite, was the home of John Wharf. When he died it became the property of his daughter "Poll," or Polly Boynton. Her son sold it to the elder Tracy, who tore it down. Mrs. Boynton later married Oliver Younger. She was thus the ancestor of many of the Boyntons and Youngers of to-day.

Immediately adjoining the Wharf house was the Tristram Coffin house, remembered by many old people. Becky Rich lived where the piggery, at the foot of gravel hill, is now located. She, like many others, of the fraternity of Dogtown, told fortunes by means of coffee grounds. After Mrs. Day was married, she recalls going over to Aunt Rich's and having her tell of her beau "clear across the water." She says Aunt Becky was a nice old woman, but that little reliance was placed in her forecasts.

Opposite Becky Rich was the house of Nathaniel Day. He was the son of Anthony Day, and married Mary Davis. He became the father of seventeen children, among them three pairs of twins. His son Isaac was a gunner on the frigate Constitution, now laid up at Portsmouth. A man named Liscomb at one time lived in one side of this old Day house. Eben Day, of Reynard street, as well as his brother, was born in this house, and all played about the streets of Dogtown in their boyhood. It stood just beyond the barn, which is now there. The cellar has long been filled up.

At Brown's Plain, half way over the back road toward the Castle, lived Molly Miller. Later she lived at the Harbor on Back street, where Mr. Day recalls seeing her after she had become insane, fastened in her room with a clothes-stick. Next on the left was the house of a man named Emmons.

At one time in her life Aunt Rachel Smith, daughter of Becky Rich, lived in the Castle. Later she lived in the house a little further on the back road from Molly Miller's. It was up on the hill, and the cellar remains. Then with her mother she went to Dogtown street, and lived in the Easter Carter house. After that she returned to the house on the hill. Here her son, Jack Bishop Smith, killed himself, and Aunt Rachel's sorrow over her loss is still vividly recalled.

"Aunt Smith" used to make a "dire drink," brewed from foxberry leaves, spruce tops, and other botanical specimens, which she was wont to peddle in the village, saying as she entered a house, "Now, ducky, I've come down to bring a dire drink, for I know you feel springish."

There were never many houses along this portion of the back road. Between the point where it met the Dogtown Commons road and the Castle stood the house of old Uncle Daniel Tucker, whose daughter Dorcas—"Dark Tucker," as she was called—nursed Judith Ryon in her last sickness.

It has always seemed to me that this back road more closely resembles the Scottish moors, as we read of them, than any portion of the Commons. About half way across to the Dogtown road formerly stood three houses in a row, while another stood on the opposite side. These houses were located where the boys now play ball, "Brown's Plain," as it is called.

CHAPTER IV.

IN DOGTOWN VILLAGE.

It is quite a little walk from the house of Becky Rich, on the back road, up gravel hill, to the Vivian barn. This barn is a landmark. When one reaches this point he is quite ready to enjoy the historic spots that lie before him. A few rods beyond the barn the road makes an abrupt turn and almost winds back upon itself. Just at this turn, on the right, is a split ledge, making a break in the stone wall that outlines the road. Into this crack in the ledge, a few years since, a misguided cow wandered. No human ingenuity was capable of getting her out alive. Directly opposite is the site of the home of a man named Clark. The cellar on the left, beyond the barn, which looks so much like a pile of rocks in a hollow, is that of Henry Davis. It is directly in the road, the yard not being walled.

The road, which has descended from the Vivian barn to this place, here begins to rise, and when it reaches a point a few rods further, where a fine view of Ipswich Bay, the Newburyport shore, and the West Gloucester hills is obtainable, the most celebrated cellar of Dogtown is seen. This is the reputed home of John Morgan Stanwood, who was many years ago made immortal by the muse of Hiram Rich in the pages of the *Atlantic*. It may be well for one to seat himself on the moss-covered door-stone and recall the lines :

> " Morgan Stanwood, patriot :
> Little more is known ;
> Nothing of his home is left
> But the door-step stone.

> " Morgan Stanwood, to our thought
> You return once more :
> Once again the meadows lift
> Daisies to your door.

> " Once again the morn is sweet,
> Half the hay is down :—
> Hark ! what means that sudden clang
> From the distant town ?

"Larum bell and rolling drum
        Answer sea-borne guns;
Larum bell and rolling drum
        Summon Freedom's sons!

"And the mower thinks to him
        Cry both bell and drum.
'Morgan Stanwood, where art thou?
        Here th' invaders come.'

"Morgan Stanwood needs no more
        Bell and drum beat call;
He is one who, hearing once,
        Answers once for all.

"Ne'er the mower murmured then,
        Half my grass is mown,
Homespun isn't soldier wear,
        Each may save his own.'

"Fallen scythe and aftermath
        Lie forgotten now;
Winter needs may come and find
        But a barren mow.

"Down the musket comes. 'Good wife
        Wife, a quicker flint!'
And the face that questions face
        Hath no color in 't.

"'Wife, if I am late to-night,
        Milk the heifer first;
Ruth, if I'm not home at all,
        Worst has come to worst!'

"Morgan Stanwood sped along,
        Not the common road;
Over wall and hill-top straight,
        Straight for death, he strode;

" Leaving her to hear at night
        Tread of burdened men,
    By the gate and through the gate,
        At the door, and then—

" Ever after that to hear,
        When the grass is sweet,
    Through the gate and through the night,
        Slowly coming feet.

" Morgan Stanwood's roof is gone:
        Here the door-step lies:

One may stand and think and think,—
        For the thought will rise,

" Were we where the meadow was,
        Mowing grass alone,
    Would we go the way he went,
        From this very stone?

" Were we on the door-step here,
        Parting for a day,
    Would we utter words as though
        Parting were for aye?

" Would we?   Heart, the hearth is dear,
        Meadow-math is sweet:
    Parting be as parting may,
        After all, we meet.

John Morgan Stanwood was the son of Nehemiah and Ruth (Morgan) Stanwood. The parish records show that he was baptized August 7, 1774. The poem evidently did not refer to a Revolutionary experience. He died October 30, 1852, aged 78. These dates so perplexed me, notwithstanding the tradition that Stanwood came back from the war a cripple, and the further fact that the children of Mrs. Dade, once a resident of the village, had handed down her stories of the exploits of "Morgan Stannard," that I asked Mr. Rich his authority for the poem. He candidly confessed that although he wrote the lines with the full belief that Morgan Stanwood was the hero of Rowe's Bank, Mr. Babson, the historian, later convinced him that Peter Lurvey, of Dogtown Commons, and not Stanwood, was the man who should have been immortalized.

It is quite evident, also, that Stanwood did not live in the house with the "door-step stone," for this is the cellar of John Clark, who resided there within the memory of men now living. This house, like most of those remaining in the early part of the century, was a small structure, perhaps 15x35, standing side to the road, with a door in the middle, and with an ordinary pitched roof. The cellars, which are generally 15 feet square, were under only one end of the houses. The Clark house became so decrepit that it was torn down in 1820. Clark must have died a short time before this date. His wife and children removed to the Harbor.

The next cellar on the left of the road is that of Philip Priestly, who is remembered as a hearty old man of 70, climbing a locust tree to view the festivities of the Harrison hard cider campaign in 1840. Nathaniel Babson, who helped tear down the Clark house, was formerly engaged in the freighting business from Gloucester to Boston, and Priestly was one of his crew. Several persons who were born in this house, I am told, are still living. Priestly died Nov. 27, 1845, of consumption, at the age of 75.

Philip Priestly was the father of quite a family of children. One of these was Philip Priestly, well remembered in Gloucester, another was Mrs. Hannah Curtis; Eliza, who married Joseph Greenleaf; Ann, who married a Smith; and Jane. Philip's wife was Naomi Clark.

Opposite John Clark's house, already mentioned, was the home of William Pulcifer. Between Clark's and Philip Priestly's are two cellars, which some have incorrectly assumed were of farm buildings. If the house with the doorstone is not Clark's—some deny it—one of these is his. The other is that of Arthur Wharf, son of Abraham, the suicide.

A large yard, enclosed by a stone wall, marks the
site of the next house. Here lived Joseph Stevens,
one of the most enterprising of the farmers of the
village. I judge him to be the son of another Joseph,
from the record of his baptism, Aug. 17, 1763. There
is a large collection of foundation stones at this point,
showing the location of the barn, with a passage
leading to it from the house, the big shed for wagons,
and the sheep pen. He kept more stock than any
other man in the settlement. He laid claim to more
land than any of his neighbors, and kept a good team,
which was often in demand. His character is not
highly spoken of, however, by those who recall him.

I am told by old residents of Riverdale that they
well remember when the children of Joseph Stevens
used to go to school in the old schoolhouse by the
mill.

Directly opposite Stevens' house, on a knoll, stood
the house of perhaps the most celebrated character in
the village, Esther (or as she was commonly called,
"Easter") Carter. No cellar marks the spot, for
there was none under it. It was the only two-story
house standing in Dogtown, within the memory of
any person now living. It was clapboarded, and the
boards were fastened on with wooden pegs. A man
who helped pull down the structure tells me he kept

a number of the pegs as souvenirs for quite a while. Easter Carter was living in 1833. She was very poor, and it was a common custom for the young people of Riverdale and Annisquam to make excursions to her house, taking their lunches, and getting her to boil cabbage for them. The "cabbage dinner" partaken in picnic style, is still one of the popular institutions of Cape Ann. Easter Carter would tell the fortunes of the young people, doubtless linking their lives together in their forecasts in a way acceptable to the romantic. The walk home in the moonlight would be something to remember, as those Appalachians who have crossed the weird Dogtown pastures by moonlight in later years can testify. One staid old citizen recently informed me he had "often been up there with a parcel of girls."

Easter Carter was poor, but quite respectable, and undeserving of the distinction which classes her with other Dogtown dames of doubtful reputation. She was a single woman, and though pinched by poverty, very aristocratic. She did not like to have people think she, like some of her neighbors, subsisted on berries in the summer time. "I eats no trash," she remarked to a suggestion at one time. One bright Sunday afternoon the parents of David Dennison, with their small boy, went on a walk to the pastures, turning in by Easter Carter's house. He remembers that as they passed, she, divining that they were to pluck berries as refreshment, remarked, " The berries seem to hide this year."

Easter Carter was noted as a nurse. It is thought by the venerable Eli Morgan of Lanesville that Easter and her brother William came here from England, which accounts for the silence of the town and parish records concerning them. He says Joseph, a son of William and Annie, lived a long time in Lanesville.

I have said that Easter Carter was perfectly respectable, as well as aristocratic, and this character may to some have seemed incompatible with other statements. I have been somewhat mystified about it myself. The truth seems to be that when Easter Carter was dead, and the house of Becky Rich on the back road had become too dilapidated for occupancy, she was taken up, bag and baggage, and installed in Easter's house. Becky had a daughter, Rachel, widow of Thomas Smith, who went with her. It appears that the woman who told fortunes, boiled cabbage, baked Johnny cake, and made life merry for all the youth who visited her, was not Easter Carter, nor Becky Rich, but Rachel Smith. I am very positive that there are old men living now who as youths used to go up to Granny Rich's, but who have confused her name with that of Easter Carter because of the house. While it is admitted that many of the scenes of festivity connected with it occurred when Becky Rich lived there, it is insisted by people who must know because they were there, that Easter, too, was wont to entertain the young people in it. At one time a party of young people collected a lot of wall paper —each bringing any pieces they had on hand—and went up and papered Easter's premises, the harlequin effect being quite pleasing to her, apparently.

Dogtown people had, as a rule, little use for but one story of a dwelling, and perhaps that was the reason that the upper floor of Easter's house was occupied by one of the most singular characters of the village. This was "Old Ruth." She was a mulatto, and doubtless was one of the manumitted slaves that abounded in Gloucester early in the century.

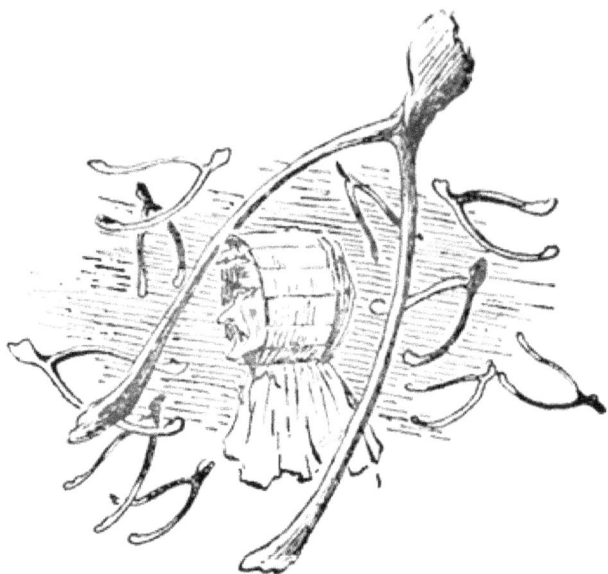

A "WISHBONE" BONNET.

CHAPTER V.

"OLD RUTH AND GRANNY DAY."

The old Ellery House, at the Green, formerly the parsonage of the first parish church, which stood behind it on the Green, and one of the finest samples of provincial or colonial architecture in existence in New England, at one time had, if it does not have to-day, a slave pen under its roof. In the fine old gambrel-roofed mansion owned by Gustavus Babson, across the highway from the Ellery house, there is another. To whom "Old Ruth" belonged I cannot find out. She went by the name of " Tie," and also was known as " John Woodman."

The masculine cognomen fitted her better than the gentle name of Ruth, for until the closing days of her life she was never known to dress in feminine apparel. Perhaps she was the original " new woman." She was accustomed to doing a man's work, and dressed in men's clothing. Building stone walls and such heavy toil were her chief employments. She used to say that she worked out of doors when she was young because she had to do it, and that she wore men's clothing for the same reason, until she came to prefer it. When she was taken to the poor-house, she was obliged to conform to the customs of civilization and put on skirts. A ledge beyond Easter Carter's still bears the name, " Ruth's Ledge," in her honor.

In a small hut in the same enclosure with Easter Carter's house lived Molly Stevens, old " Joe Stevens' " sister. No one keeps her memory green. She must have made life very unhappy for the gentle Easter, unless history is at fault.

Directly beyond this site, a pair of bars opening into the yard, and a big bowlder standing as a sentinel in front, is the cellar of Annie Carter, wife of William, Easter Carter's brother, a record of whose baptism I find in the Fourth Parish, April 1, 1776. This

was the last house taken down in the village. For
some reason the place was always known as Annie's.
After her death, William, with the children, moved
away. Annie was known as "Granny Carter," and
is said to have been a "little small woman."

One or two other cellars which I have not identified with former occupants, lie across the road from
Annie Carter's, and two, together with a potato hole
that may deceive the uninitiated, lie between it and
the cellar, on a rise of ground, formerly under the
house, it is alleged, of Moll Jacobs. I am somewhat
disposed to think that this cellar is that of the house
of good Deacon Winslow, who lived either here or
very near it. Nobody can remember where Molly
lived before taking up her abode in the Lurvey house,
of which we shall speak later.

In an enclosure at this point are a number of small
bowlders, marked, "First Attack," etc., that are likely
to mystify the visitor. One is marked, "James Merry
died, Sept. 10, 1892." Mr. Merry was gored to death
by a bull, his dead body being found by the rock
bearing the second inscription. William A. Hodgkins of Riverdale once gave the writer and a party
of friends a very graphic description of this tragedy,
as they stood at the spot. The marks were placed by
Raymond P. Tarr and D. K. Goodwin, about a week
after the death of Mr. Merry.

The Fifth Parish records say that "Moley Jakups, daughter of Isack and Molly, was baptized Jan. 31, 1763." Molly and Judy Rhines, with others, seem to have done a great deal to give to Dogtown a reputation which also was undeservedly conferred on Gloucester as a whole, so that the favored residents of Rockport were led for a generation to look down on a native of the larger place. No traditions, except those of a rather unsavory reputation, remain of Molly.

Almost opposite the Jacobs cellar, on the left of the road, is a well marked cellar, said to be all that remains of the home of Dorcas Foster. She was eight years old at the commencement of the Revolutionary war, having been born at the Harbor village. Her father left his family in this house for safety from the British, whom he feared might come and sack the town, and went to the war. George Wonson, who lived with his grandmother when a boy, recalls many of her stories of life in those troublous times.

Abram Wharf she always referred to as "Neighbor Wharf," and called his wife "Aunt Wharf." The children used to be sent to the harbor village for supplies, and were accustomed to pay one dollar for a pound of tea, and for other necessary things in proportion. Little Dorcas naturally feared the British, sharing the terror which led to the growth of Dogtown, and one day when she saw seven soldiers, she started to run, without considering whether they were British or Continentals. She was reassured by one of them, who told her not to be frightened, as they would not hurt her. Her experience well illustrates the hardships of those and even later days, suffered by the brave residents of Cape Ann.

Ezekiel W. Chard tells me that in the embargo times the women of 'Squam would walk as far as Ipswich, going across the beach, to get a half bushel of meal, the distance being twelve miles. In those days it was very rare to get either bread or cake, he says.

Dorcas Foster was three times married, her first husband being an Oakes, the second a Stevens, and the last Capt. Joseph Smith, who commanded a privateer in the war of 1812. George Wonson is a son of Louisa Smith, their daughter. She has many descendants in Gloucester. Most of her life was spent in the ancient house which until lately stood on the rock at the corner of Prospect and Warner streets, where the home of M. H. Perkins is now located.

Not far beyond the Foster cellar, on the same side of the road, is one which has been recently filled with rocks. It would be unwise to disturb them, for the cellar is the tomb of several horses, which have been

shot as a matter of mercy, after having been turned
out in the pastures to die. This is all that remains
of the home of Capt. Isaac Dade. He, too, has
descendants both in Gloucester and Rockport.

Mrs. H. G. Wetherbee, his granddaughter, fur-
nishes me the following particulars of the life of Isaac
Dade:

"Isaac Dade, while a school boy in or near Lon-
don, England, was impressed on board an English
man-of-war. During the Revolution his vessel was
anchored off Gloucester, and it became his duty to
row one of the officers ashore. While doing so he
noticed a fishing vessel ready to sail. As soon as
the officer was landed he lost no time getting aboard
the vessel. She was bound to Virginia with a cargo
of fish. When he reached there he joined the Conti-
nental army, and was later in three memorable engage-
ments. He was at Yorktown when Lord Cornwallis
surrendered. He was wounded in battle, receiving
a sabre cut across the back of his neck, which crip-
pled him for life.

"After the war he married a Southern lady by the
name of Fanny Brundle. Her father's plantation
adjoined that of the mother of Washington. She was
on intimate terms with the Washingtons. Two children were born to them in Virginia. His health

began to fail, and he remembered Gloucester, and went there hoping that the change of life would be beneficial—intending to return to Virginia the following autumn. He did not, however, but spent the rest of his life there. He kept a fish market in Gloucester under great disadvantages, as the women preferred to get the fish from the boats as they came in. During his life he received no pension, but after his death it was paid to his widow."

This story points to the visit of the Falcon, later mentioned in connection with Peter Lurvey's bravery, as the probable time when Isaac Dade decided to make America his home. I have already indicated the probable site of his Dogtown domicile. The theory that he came in the Falcon is strengthened by the fact that in 1775—the same year of Capt. Lindsay's attack—two vessels were dispatched from Gloucester to Virginia for supplies, owing to the poverty of the people on Cape Ann.

It must have been a great deal of a change to this high-spirited maiden to begin her married life in a region so barren, so lonely, as Dogtown; but love for her husband must have sweetened the bitterness, for she was never heard to complain.

Directly beyond this cellar on the left is a swamp, which has for many decades been a slough of despond for cattle and horses. It is always the repository of one or more unfortunates, which have got in but could never get out. This is "Granny Day's swamp." Her cellar is covered by water at the corner of it. She was a school teacher, and one of her pupils was Nathaniel Day, the patriarch. Near here is Whetstone Rock, a natural curiosity, so hollowed out that it served the purpose indicated. Some curiosity seeker split it off and carried it away a few years since.

COUNCIL OF THE CROWS.

CHAPTER VI.

PETER LURVEY AND "BLACK NEIL."

The only resident of Dogtown mentioned in Babson's History of Gloucester, was Abraham Wharf, who lived in a large gambrel-roofed house near the junction of the two roads of the village, not over a mile from the "Whale's Jaw," and who according to the historian, lonely and weary, crawled under a rock near by and committed suicide, in 1814. At that time there were at least six other houses in Dogtown occupied. The last inhabitant of the village was a colored man called "Neil"—his name was Cornelius Finson—who lived on the road leading from Gee avenue in Riverdale to Dogtown, in the house of Judith Ryon, called by all old-timers, "Judy Rhines." He was a man of intelligence, evidently, for Ezekiel W. Chard remembers him as a clerk for the boat fishers of 'Squam. Others recall him as principally engaged in the more prosaic calling of an executioner of hogs.

He was closely acquainted both with Judy Rhines and Molly Jacobs. He was firmly persuaded that when Molly Jacobs died she left buried treasure in her cellar, and it was with difficulty he could be kept away from the quite uninhabitable hole. Long after Judy Rhines was dead he lingered around her house, until its walls fell in, when he sought refuge in the cellar. From this, cold, dirty, half-starved, and shaking with the combined infirmity of old age and fright, he was taken on a bitter day in winter, 1830, by Constable William Tucker of Riverdale—the people of that village having complained of the case to the Overseers of the Poor—and carried off to the almshouse. As they passed the store of John Low Babson, near the Poles on Washington street, they stopped and Neil was taken in for a half hour to get warm. Mr. Babson gave him some tobacco. After Neil had gone, Mark Allen, sitting in the store, said, "There, I'll bet he'll be so comfortable at the poor-house that he won't live a week." He was right. Within seven days Neil was dead.

If the reader will now start at either Gee avenue

or Stanwood street past the old Langsford house and the "Castle," over the Commons road to the Morgan brook, just beyond the "Castle," and thence follow the road along until, if it is the wet season, he comes to another brook crossing the road on higher ground, he will soon notice at the left what is known as "Beech Pasture." A high hill is in the pasture, from the top of which is obtained a fine view of Annisquam and Ipswich Bay. On this hill, quite a distance from the road, is a cellar. Near it is a lilac bush and also, as in the case of many cellars, a gooseberry bush. This is the site of what, taken all together, is the most famous of the houses. First of all it was the home of Peter Lurvey. I have already said that he was the hero of the episode commemorated by Hiram Rich in "Morgan Stanwood." Babson says his father, Peter Lurvey, removed from Ipswich to Gloucester in 1707. In 1710 he married Rachel Elwell, and our Peter was one of eight sons, the elder Peter being ancestor of all the Lurveys in Gloucester.

Peter Lurvey, the Revolutionary patriot, married a sister of Abraham Wharf, who lived in the next house beyond. On August 8, 1775, the British sloop-of-war Falcon, which had assisted in the capture of Bunker Hill, chased a Salem schooner into Gloucester harbor, where she grounded on the flats between

Pearce's wharf and Five Pound Island. Capt. Lindsay of the Falcon attempted to board her with several barge loads of marines. The people of Gloucester, an alarm having been given, hauled two swivel guns to a point opposite Vincent's Cove, and with the aid of muskets prevented a capture. Then Lindsay, full of wrath, cannonaded the town (one shot hitting the First Parish Church, where it is now suspended in the vestry) and landed men at Fort Point to fire the village. The firing party were made prisoners, and the boarding party were also captured by the intrepid villagers. In the engagement Benjamin Rowe was instantly killed and Peter Lurvey mortally wounded.

The above is the story substantially as told by Babson and Pringle. It is one side of the picture. I will now give the other, as handed down by his wife and daughter, and related to me by his descendants. On that fatal morning Lurvey, his wife and little Mary Millett—afterwards Mary Riggs—were over on Pearce's Island huckleberrying. Hearing the alarm, Peter Lurvey bade his wife good-by, hurriedly rowed across to the other shore, ran up to the house, and got his gun, thence across the fields and pastures to the Harbor Village, where he met his death. For some quite unexplainable reason his face was never seen again by his wife and children. It was never known

what became of his body. Our progenitors were
peculiar about such things. My great-grandmother
used to tell of her grandfather, killed at the battle
of Menotomy, as the British were returning from
Lexington on April 19, 1775. His body was immediately buried, in a grave with Jason Russell and ten
others—now in the Arlington cemetery—and all his
children ever saw again was his old farmer's hat,
reserved for identification.

Mrs. Lurvey lived to be 104 years old, and is
remembered by people yet living. I have referred to
her as a sister to Abraham Wharf. Whether she
was the sister who was with him at the time he committed suicide no person can now tell. It was in
1814. Wharf sat by the fire sharpening his razor.
"Sister," said he, do you think people who commit
suicide go to heaven?" "I don't know; but I hope
you will never do such a thing, brother," was her
answer. "God forbid," was his solemn response.
Soon he slipped the razor into his shoe, unobserved,
and went out. A little later he was found with his
throat cut, dead.

The explanation of Mr. Rich's confusing Lurvey
and Morgan Stanwood is that John Morgan Stanwood
married Lurvey's daughter. Until the time that Mrs.
Lurvey died they seemed to have lived with her in this

THE WITCHES' FLIGHT.

house. Later they moved to the house by the Morgan brook, where I think Ruth Morgan, his mother, and probably Morgan Stanwood himself, were born. But more of this later. After the Stanwoods left the house, which was by this time getting old and weather-beaten, Molly Jacobs, with her friends Sarah Phipps —more often than not called Sally Jacobs—and Mrs. Stanley left the house they had been living in—perhaps that already indicated on the Dogtown road— and came here, by the invitation of "Grandther Stannard." The latter women's grandson, "Sammy Stanley," lived with them and took care of them. Mrs. Almira Riggs of Riverdale, a granddaughter of Morgan Stanwood, told me before her death that she often as a child used to go up to this Lurvey house in winter with food for the old people, and would find them in bed, the coverlet white with snow where the wind had sifted through in the night. After a time the trio of old ladies were taken off to the poor house, where they died. Molly Jacobs was smarter than Sarah Phipps. Sarah would get mad at Molly, and say: "I shan't tell you where I hid the keerds. I hid them behind the old chest, but I shan't tell you."

"Sammy Stanley's" real name was Sam Maskey. He was always brought up by his grandmother to do housework. He went about with a handkerchief tied

over his head and did woman's work in preference to
any other. In fact, though he wore men's clothes he
had been brought up a girl. After his aged relative
was taken off his hands, he moved to Rockport, where
he went out washing for a livelihood, and laid up
money, so that when he died he was quite a stock-
holder in the cotton mills.

The history of the Lurvey house is nearly finished.
Just before Mollie Jacobs went to the almshouse,
"Black Neil" Finson, coming from some other house
he had inhabited, moved here. The only place he
could well stay in was the cellar, which he made
water tight by boarding over the first floor. I have
already said he thought there was money there. In
the course of time, his friend Judy Rhines living in
the next house toward the Castle on the same side the
Common road, took pity on him, and invited him to
occupy the empty part of her dwelling.

To return for a moment to Lurvey. As one walks
or rides through Washington street in Riverdale,
coming from the harbor, just after he crosses the
bridge, he notices on the right, the second house from
Reynard street, a two-story structure with pitched
roof, still in excellent repair, and looking like anything but a historic mansion. Yet this house, recon-
structed to be sure, was successively the home of Peter

Lurvey and his family. Morgan Stanwood, Molly Jacobs and her two unfortunate companions, who lived in it in company with Black Neil and Sammy Stanley, as already related. In some way or other it became the property of a man named Whipple living in the vicinity, who sold it when it was but a skeleton, to Isaac and Reuben Day. They had it taken down, and it was found that the oak frame was perfectly intact.

The Day brothers therefore had the material taken to the present site, and the house was rebuilt, the old frame being used in its entirety. There it stands, a monument to the hero and martyr of the Falcon fight, and there it seems likely to remain another century at least, for it is perfectly sound. I have these facts on the authority of several of Isaac Day's descendants, as well as of James Thurston of Riverdale, who helped take it down, and was one of the mechanics who rebuilt it. Mr. Eben Day of Reynard street spent several days cleaning bricks from its chimneys when it was demolished, he tells me.

It seems rather mysterious that Black Neil, who lived in it when Molly and Sarah and Mrs. Stanley were taken to the almshouse, was not taken too, for at that time the roof had caved in and was in a wretched condition. Old people in Riverdale have

had it pointed out to them for nearly two generations
as the house where Black Neil once lived, but even
those who furnished me the information as to its
identity were surprised to know that it was the Lurvey
house.

CHAPTER VII.

"JUDY RHINES" AND "JOHNNY MORGAN."

The Judy Rhines house, too, was caved in as to its roof, it seems, when Black Neil removed thither from his former dwelling. And this circumstance probably explains why "Liz" Tucker, its owner and former occupant, left the society of her niece Judy, and sought a home near the harbor where she died. The house where she died stood exactly where the entrance to Oak Grove cemetery is now located. Judy's house was a double one. It will be noticed by the visitor to the spot that there are two cellars. It seems that Lizzie (or "Liz") Tucker, was Judith Ryon's aunt, and therefore must have been a sister to

either her father Patrick Ryon, an Irishman, or to her
mother, a daughter of William Riggs. Liz Tucker
lived in one part of the house, but was dead, doubtless,
at the time Judy extended the hospitalities of the place
to Neil Finson.

How long the two were tenants of the place I am
unable to say. The house was one of the favorite
haunts of young people on holidays, and was so at the
time both lived there. Judy was a tall, rawboned
woman, who had great courage. If she told a person
approaching her house to stand still, they would not
move any nearer. She had many friends. One of
the places she visited, according to Benjamin Rowe
Kidder of Rockport, was "Uncle Miah" Knowlton's,
for whom he worked. Aunt Knowlton used to load
her up with fish and tea. The young people of that
day refuse to admit that she was in any sense a witch,
or so considered. After Judy died, as before related,
Neil lived in the house until the only place he could
stay was in the cellar. He was a big powerful negro,
with very prominent protruding teeth. At the time he
was taken from the cellar to the poor house, it was
full of ice, and his toes were some of them frozen.

"Judy Rhines," as she is called, was baptized
Dec. 30, 1771, at the Sandy Bay parish church. She
was living in 1830, nine years before the death of her

colored friend "Neil" Finson. She gained a precarious living, like her friends Mollie Jacobs, Easter Carter and Tammy Younger, by picking berries, telling fortunes. and in other ways. One day she went into Mr. Babson's store at the Poles, and bought some groceries. She tendered in payment a $5 bill, a note on the old United States bank. It was the only one Mr. Babson had ever seen. "I don't think I want this." he said. "It is just as good as any," she replied; "I took it for pasture rent from Mr. Whipple." He finally took it, and on presentation at the Gloucester Bank found she was right. It was on a branch of the bank for the state of Georgia.

Years ago. in the Gloucester *Telegraph*, some antiquarian told a story of what might have been his own experience. He said two boys who considered the poultry and chattels of a "witch" public property, stole from Judith Ryon a couple of geese. They were safely away, as they thought, when they heard Judy coming brandishing a hoe, and screeching,

"Now, ye hell birds, I've got ye!" The response was a goose, plump in her face, and the asseveration, "No you haint." Prostrated by the foul assault, Judy lay senseless, while the boys again securing their prey, vanished.

As we seem to have turned back toward the Castle, we may as well continue, and more particularly examine the territory around Morgan's brook, or the "Slough," as it is more often called. In the early days of this century, some sixteen or twenty men used to go over this road to general training, their homes being between the Castle and Dogtown.

Over these pastures, on either side, many sheep were wont to graze a century ago. Abraham Wharf, in his palmy days, kept lots of them. On the opposite side of the road from Judy Rhines', just by the brook, is the cellar of the dwelling of "Jim" White. I can find little about him. Morgan's brook is a discouraging place to cross. If one confines himself to the stepping stones on the left, going toward Riverdale, or on the right, proceeding the other way, it can be crossed without wetting one's feet. The stranger is likely to attempt the other side, and come to grief.

After crossing the brook, on the same side as Judy Rhines' cellar, one sees a big bowlder, beside the road.   Right against it, on one side, are the foundations of a small building, while in the yard with this, enclosed by a wall, are the remains of a larger structure.   The building by the rock was the hut in which John Morgan Stanwood spent his last days.   Mr. Rich, in his poem, dropped the John, while the custom of his contemporaries was to drop the Stanwood.   It is a painful but well-authenticated fact, that he was known to some, as long as he lived, as "Johnny Morgan."   Of course he was not that Johnny who played the organ, nor the estimable gentleman who caters to the finer taste of the present generation of Gloucester people.

I misspent many precious hours trying, first to find if John Morgan Stanwood was the man I was hunting after, and second, seeking to find out who the Morgan was who lived by the brook.   That this was not strange may be understood, when I say that a lady still living told me that for years she went to school, and was intimate with "Nabby Morgan," his daughter, before the person told her that her name was really Abigail Morgan Stanwood.

Morgan Stanwood never went to the wars, so those who knew him as Capt. Morgan Stanwood made a mistake if they thought the title a military one.   During the Revolutionary war, or a little later, he went on foreign voyages. He married Mary Lurvey, and had many children. "Granther Stannard," or "Johnny Morgan," as you will, seems thoroughly to have enjoyed life on Dogtown Common. He spent his later years cobbling shoes. This work he did at first in a little addition to his house, which was then and has ever since borne the name of "The Boo."

After his wife died, and his children grew up, the confusion of so many in the house, and the fact that they had so many callers among their young acquaintances, so disturbed his mind, that he sought relief by building the hut under the rock. Many living recall this cosy corner, where he peacefully cobbled shoes for the remainder of his days. On a shelf in the corner he kept a book in which he made a record of the interesting matters that came to his notice. I should like to get hold of that book. For a year I chased after such a journal of life in Dogtown, that I finally found never existed; but I have no doubt of the existence of this, though it probably has long since gone to decay. Stanwood has several grandchildren living.

Lest I forget it, let me say here that Morgan Stanwood's old "boo"—it was a booth, built of slabs and covered with turf, Mrs. Rachel Day says—was standing when the war of the Rebellion begun, but old

THE "OLD CASTLE."

soldiers who left it when they marched, found it gone on their return.

The "Castle" is now owned by Mrs. Mary A. Riggs, a sprightly old lady of 80, who lives on the main road in Riverdale. Some of the Lufkin family seem to have lived in it during its early history. It came to Mrs. Riggs through her father, Capt. Sam. Riggs, of whom it used to be said that he could walk from the old Riggs house in Riverdale to Rockport without getting off from his own land. The Riggs house is quite near the Castle, though on another road near Goose Cove. It is supposed that that part of it which is constructed of square logs was built by Thos. Riggs, the first school master and town clerk, in 1661. His grandson, George Riggs, built the gambrel roof portion. It is undoubtedly the oldest house on the Cape. Thomas was the progenitor of all the Riggs family of Gloucester. Mrs. Riggs, mentioned above, used to go to school to Judy Millett.

The "old castle" is a restored gambrel roof, and seems likely to remain for another century as a good sample of the better class of Dogtown dwellings.

It seems probable that Hetty Balch lived in this vicinity, but of this I would like further proof. Possibly she lived in the village. It is but five minutes walk from "Johnny Morgan's Boo," and the Castle to the electrics in Riverdale.

CHAPTER VIII.

CONCLUSION.

If it happens that one has not turned off from the main Dogtown road, at Granny Day's swamp, he will keep on over a slight elevation, past the crossing of the Pigeon Cove path, which really is for some distance in the road, until he reaches the Whale's Jaw.

Soon after passing Whale's Jaw, the road, almost obliterated by time and changes of ownership in the pastures, reaches Revere street, the old Sandy Bay road already referred to. On the Pigeon Cove path, a little distance beyond the Whale's Jaw, are the graves of old Mr. Blance and wife, marked by rude head and foot stones picked out from the rocks which bestrew the Commons. Their cellar is near Pigeon Hill, on the path from Pigeon Cove to the Whale's Jaw. It was known as "Blance's" to two generations. The cleared land made a fine place for the boys of fifty years since to go from Lanesville and Pigeon Cove on Fast Day to play ball.

In Dogtown, almost or rather near it, over the ridge toward Alewife brook, is the cellar of the house in which Col. William Pearce, one of the wealthiest men of old Gloucester, sought refuge from marauding expeditions in war times. He kept great numbers of sheep. Mr. Chard, almost a centenarian, picturesquely describes a scene of his boyhood, during the war of 1812. He woke one morning and was summoned into the garden of the house on the banks of Lobster Cove, in which he was born, and still lives. Secured to a rock directly across the cove, still to be seen, were several British barges, belonging to a war vessel anchored by the bar in the harbor of Annisquam. Coming down the hill towards the boats was a negro, bearing on his back his booty in the shape of one of Col. Pearce's black sheep.

I have speculated somewhat concerning the reason for Babson's reticence in his history concerning Dogtown and its people. His history was published forty years ago. The village degenerated as it grew old, and the Dogtown familiar to him in his younger days was not a place to inspire great enthusiasm. At the time he wrote less than twenty years had passed since "Black

Nell," Molly Jacobs, Annie Carter and others had died. Many of their connections were still living, and to speak as freely as one can to-day of the village would have caused more or less strife. Had my friend Pringle had more time, he might have included the story of Dogtown in his interesting centennial history, but the omission was quite excusable when the magnitude of the task he set himself is considered.

I find that I have omitted the story of Peg Wesson from this narrative, though her name has been mentioned. She lived in the "Garrison House" on Prospect street, opposite Dale avenue. It now stands on Maplewood avenue. She is the only reputed witch of Cape Ann of whom it can be alleged, with history to endorse the allegation, that she rode on a broomstick. Shortly before departing for the siege of Louisburg, Babson says, several of Capt. Byles' company visited Peg, and so exasperated her that she threatened to visit them in wrath at Cape Breton. While camping before Louisburg, the attention of the Gloucester men was attracted by the peculiar performances of a crow which circled just above them. Several unsuccessful efforts were made to shoot the bird of ill omen. Finally a soldier suggested that it must be Peg supernaturally transformed into a crow. If it was the witch, nothing but a bullet cast from silver or gold would be sufficiently potent to puncture her. A silver sleeve button was rammed into a gun, and fired, the bird falling with a hurt leg. On their return to Gloucester, the soldiers were interested to learn that at the precise time the crow was wounded, Peg fell (of course from her broomstick), with a fracture of her leg, and the doctor, on dressing the wound, extracted the identical silver button therefrom. Many of the inhabitants of Gloucester of those days believed this tale.

Much more of a descriptive nature might be written concerning the old, deserted village. If there is more extant of an historical nature, the writer has been unable, by persistent searching, to find it.

The best authorities claim that there are at present 41 cellars which can be found in Dogtown. Of these the writer has identified many more than he believed was possible when he began the work. He is more gratified than he can express at the general interest that has been awakened by the first publication of these notes. As aged Mr. Thurston quaintly remarks, "In old times if a person sawed a barrel in two and made two tubs, they called him a witch." This seems to be as much foundation as there is in many of the witches of Dogtown. Gloucester should cherish this ancient spot for what it has been. It is practically the only ruined city in America. I cannot close these sketches better than by following the example of Babson, and quoting Goldsmith:

"Here, as I take my solitary rounds.
Amidst thy tangled walks and ruined grounds.
And, many a year elapsed, return to view
Where once the cottage stood, the hawthorne grew.
Remembrance wakes, with all her busy train.
Swells at my breast, and turns the past to pain.

*   *   *   *   *   *   *   *

But now the sounds of population fail.
No cheerful murmurs fluctuate in the gale.
No busy steps the grass-grown footway tread.
For all the blooming flush of life is fled."

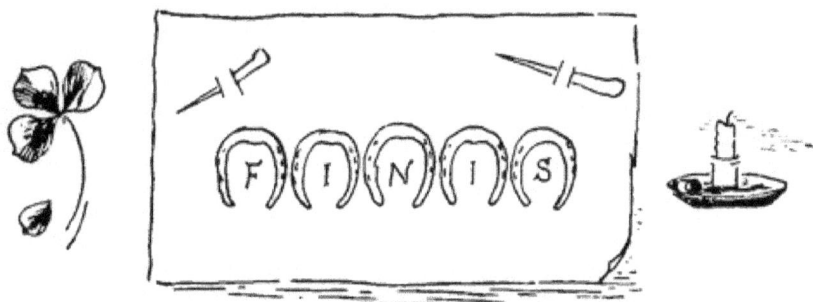

www.ingramcontent.com/pod-product-compliance
Lightning Source LLC
Chambersburg PA
CBHW021527270326
41930CB00008B/1135